TECH
bytes

HIGH-TECH

Cryptocurrency

by Kate Conley

NORWOOD HOUSE PRESS

Cover: Interest in cryptocurrencies is growing around the world.

Norwood House Press
Chicago, Illinois

For information regarding Norwood House Press, please visit our website at:
www.norwoodhousepress.com or call 866-565-2900.

PHOTO CREDITS: Cover: © Tom Stepanov/Shutterstock Images; © dennizn/Shutterstock Images, 18; © Dzelat/Shutterstock Images, 32; © EQRoy/Shutterstock Images, 15; © fizkes/Shutterstock Images, 9; © Geoffrey Swaine/Rex Features, 34; © Gorodenkoff/Shutterstock Images, 24; © juststock/iStockphoto, 5; © matejmo/iStockphoto, 6, 38; © Natnan Srisuwan/iStockphoto, 11; © NoDerog/iStockphoto, 31; © Osugi/Shutterstock Images, 42; © piccaya/iStockphoto, 36; © ronstik/iStockphoto, 23; © Shizuo Kambayashi/AP Images, 26; © South_agency/iStockphoto, 20, 28; © sunsinger/Shutterstock Images, 37; © weedezign/Shutterstock Images, 13

Content Consultant: Dr. Arthur Carvalho, Dinesh & Ila Paliwal Innovation Chair and Assistant Professor of Information Systems and Analytics, Miami University

Hardcover ISBN: 978-1-68450-918-8
Paperback ISBN: 978-1-68404-467-2

Library of Congress Cataloging-in-Publication Data

Names: Conley, Kate A., 1977- author.
Title: Cryptocurrency / Kate Conley.
Description: Chicago, IL : Norwood House Press, [2020] | Series: Tech bytes: high-tech | Audience: Grade 4 to 6. | Includes index.
Identifiers: LCCN 2018060960 (print) | LCCN 2019000306 (ebook) | ISBN 9781684044726 (ebook) | ISBN 9781684509188 (hardcover) | ISBN 9781684044672 (pbk.)
Subjects: LCSH: Cryptocurrencies--Juvenile literature. | Electronic funds transfers--Juvenile literature. | Currency question--Juvenile literature.
Classification: LCC HG1710 (ebook) | LCC HG1710 .C656 2020 (print) | DDC 332.4--dc23
LC record available at https://lccn.loc.gov/2018060960

319N_072019

Manufactured in the U   th Mankato, Minnesota.

CONTENTS

Note: Words that are **bolded** in the text are defined in the glossary.

CHAPTER 1

Bitcoin Boom

In May 2010, Laszlo Hanyecz was working as a computer programmer in Jacksonville, Florida. One evening he visited an online forum called Bitcointalk. The site drew users who were interested in a new type of digital currency called Bitcoin. At the time, it did not have any value. That's because no one had ever used it to purchase anything. But Hanyecz was curious. He wondered if it could have value in the real world.

To test his idea, Hanyecz commented on a message board. He offered to pay 10,000 bitcoins to anyone who would order two pizzas and have them delivered to his home. An anonymous computer programmer in London, England, accepted Hanyecz's offer. From London, the programmer contacted a pizza restaurant in Jacksonville, placed the order, and paid for it with a credit card. When the pizzas arrived at Hanyecz's

Before cryptocurrencies became popular, Bitcoin was mostly a fun concept for programmers.

home, he sent the programmer in London the 10,000 bitcoins.

The exchange between Hanyecz and the London programmer marked the first time in history that Bitcoin was used to make a purchase. At the time of the **transaction**, one bitcoin had a theoretical value of $0.003. So when Hanyecz received his pizzas, he spent approximately $30. Not a bad deal for either party. However, things were about to change quickly.

On July 11, 2010, a technology news site called Slashdot featured a story

As Bitcoin became popular, its worth dramatically increased.

on bitcoins. The story reached a wide audience of tech enthusiasts. Many grew excited about the potential of Bitcoin as a new type of currency. Five days after the story appeared, the value of a single bitcoin rose to $0.08. The 10,000 bitcoins Hanyecz had sent to the London programmer in May were no longer worth $30. They had risen in value. They were now worth $800.

What Is Currency?

Currency is any material that a society agrees on to use for exchanges. Early forms of currency included livestock, tobacco, grains, and cowrie shells. Over time, people created rings, **ingots**, and bars out of valuable metals to use as currency. Beginning around 650 BCE, people began to make metal into coins. Carrying around lots of coins was inconvenient. They were heavy and could be lost or stolen easily. People began using a new type of currency in the form of paper money. In 806 CE, people in China created the first paper currency. Other advances in currency, such as checks and debit cards, followed. Today, cryptocurrencies stand at the forefront of new money technology.

Digital Currency

The origins of Bitcoin go back to a person or organization known as Satoshi Nakamoto. No one knows Nakamoto's real identity, though he claimed to be a man living in Japan. In 2008, Nakamoto published an eight-page paper called "Bitcoin: A Peer-to-Peer Electronic Cash System." It explained the technology and processes needed to make a secure digital currency system work. This type of currency became known as a cryptocurrency. The next year, in 2009, the Bitcoin network began operating.

Since then, programmers have created other digital currencies based

DID YOU KNOW?

Satoshi Nakamoto owns approximately 1.1 million bitcoins, or 5 percent of all bitcoins in **circulation**. When Bitcoin's value peaked at $19,783.06 in December 2017, Nakamoto's share was worth around $20 billion.

coins, do. But cryptocurrencies and traditional currencies work differently.

In a traditional currency system, one central group controls the money. The group is usually a government. The government prints the currency. Banks accept currency from people who want to make deposits. Then, banks loan this money to other people. They charge fees to people who borrow money. The fees are how banks earn a profit. A person can also send someone else money through a bank. The bank might charge a fee here, too. This is a centralized system.

Cryptocurrency works differently. It is decentralized. It is a peer-to-peer system. That means people can accept deposits, make loans, or buy goods directly, without

on Nakamoto's ideas. More than 2,000 cryptocurrencies exist today. Some of the best known are Litecoin, Ethereum, Zcash, Dash, and Ripple. Cryptocurrencies have value in the same way that traditional currencies, such as paper bills and

Banks loan money to customers for purchases such as buying a car or a house.

using a bank or a government. This eliminates the fees that banks normally charge. It also takes power away from banks and governments. It puts the value of the currency in the hands of consumers.

Creating a Secure System

For a currency to remain valuable, people need to trust in its worth and security. To build this trust, cryptocurrencies rely on a technology called the blockchain. A blockchain is a **ledger** that records every transaction. The ledger traces the path of each unit as it is spent. This assures users that the currency is legitimate. It also prevents **fraud**, such as spending the same unit twice.

In a traditional currency system, banks keep ledgers. But with digital currencies, users keep the ledgers. Every ten minutes on average, Bitcoin software lumps transactions that have taken place during that time into a block. Users, called miners, collect transactions into blocks using the software. Each block is associated with a puzzle. Miners solve these puzzles using high-powered computers. The first to solve the puzzle broadcasts the answer and the block to all other users. The other users then **verify** the transactions inside the block. If all the transactions are valid, miners link the block to the previous one. This creates a chain of blocks, or a "blockchain," of transactions.

Ledgers help banks and other companies track how much money they have and where it goes.

Twenty-One Million Bitcoins

When Nakamoto created Bitcoin, he allowed for 21 million bitcoins to be released into circulation over the course of many years. Each time someone created a block accepted by others, new bitcoins would be released into circulation. As the number of bitcoins in circulation increased, miners would receive smaller numbers of bitcoins. This system prevents bitcoins from entering circulation too quickly and reducing their value. As of 2018, 80 percent of the bitcoins in Nakamoto's system have been released into circulation. The last 20 percent of bitcoins will take until 2140 to all be released.

Even with these safeguards, digital currency still has downsides. Its value can swing up and down in short periods. And many people distrust a system that has no central agency overseeing it. Despite these challenges, people are slowly warming up to the idea of digital currency.

More mainstream stores are accepting it as payment. And people like that the fees are very low. Cryptocurrencies have harnessed computer technology to create a new way for people to buy and sell things without traditional money.

CHAPTER 2

Everyday Uses

In 2016, digital currency enthusiast Joël Valenzuela began an experiment in Portsmouth, New Hampshire. He wanted to know if it was possible to live on only cryptocurrency. So he closed his traditional bank account. He then arranged for his employer to pay him in bitcoins. From there, he began trying to pay for things like rent, food, and gas with bitcoins.

As more businesses accept cryptocurrency, users can begin using it for everyday purchases.

"It worked very well for most of 2016," Valenzuela said, "but then transaction times and fees started to go way up. Sometimes, I would try to make a purchase, and it would take an hour to confirm. I was wandering around the store. Other times I was trying to buy something under a dollar and paying 50-cent fees. The whole thing broke down. I could no longer live this way. So I thought, do I give up? Or do I try to find a way to make it work?"

Valenzuela tried to make it work. He began looking for alternatives to Bitcoin. He settled on a new cryptocurrency called Dash. Living on Dash required some tradeoffs. His choices of restaurants became much more limited. And he had to get creative. Valenzuela found a local farmer willing to accept Dash as payment. But Valenzuela also worked for Dash. He knew getting support for problems would be easier for him, so this did make the experiment easier for Valenzuela.

Not everyone can do what Valenzuela did. That's because Portsmouth embraces cryptocurrency. Portsmouth is a

> **? DID YOU KNOW?**
>
> **Cryptocurrency has grown quickly as a payment method. In 2013, payments using Bitcoin totaled $9.8 million per month. That number had ballooned to $190.2 million per month in 2017.**

cutting-edge city. It offers more retailers per person who accept cryptocurrency than almost anywhere else in the United States. The amount of retailers who accept cryptocurrencies is the main reason Valenzuela had so much success. But a growing number of retailers around the world are accepting cryptocurrency. This increases the possibility of more people living like Valenzuela.

Portsmouth, New Hampshire, is home to many early cryptocurrency users. They had a big impact on cryptocurrencies in the small town.

Removing Regulations

In June 2017, New Hampshire governor Chris Sununu signed a bill to remove regulations from cryptocurrency in his state. Removing regulations makes it easier for businesses and consumers to trade using cryptocurrency.

Exchanges and Wallets

To begin using digital currency like Valenzuela, most people start in the same place. They need to exchange dollars for cryptocurrency. The place to do this is at a digital currency exchange. It is a virtual market where people buy, sell, and trade using digital currencies. Coinbase, Bitstamp, and Kraken are well-known exchanges. Opening an account on one of these exchanges is the first step to using digital currency.

Once a person has cryptocurrency, she must have a place to store it. With traditional currencies, people store their money in a bank. Similarly, cryptocurrency users do not store the actual money themselves. Instead, they only store a record of how many cryptocurrency units they have in a cryptocurrency wallet. It is not a physical wallet like the one a person carries in a pocket or a purse. Instead, it is a program. It runs on computers and smartphones.

A wallet comes with two important pieces of information. The first is a public key. It is a very long code that identifies the user to other users. The public key is how cryptocurrency can be sent and received. The second piece of information is a private key. It is a large, randomly generated number. The private key is secret.

Imagine that Jane and John want to make a trade. Jane wants to sell two bitcoins to John. John gives Jane his public key. That way Jane can send John his bitcoins. Jane notified the miners that she is selling two bitcoins from her wallet and that they will be going to John using his public key. Then, Jane must verify the transaction with her private key. The private key is a way for Jane to sign the transaction, and the public key verifies that it is Jane's account. When John receives the transaction, he can complete the exchange. The miners will verify the

? DID YOU KNOW?

As of 2018, 22 million Bitcoin wallets existed. That does not mean Bitcoin has 22 million users, however. Many people own multiple wallets for increased privacy.

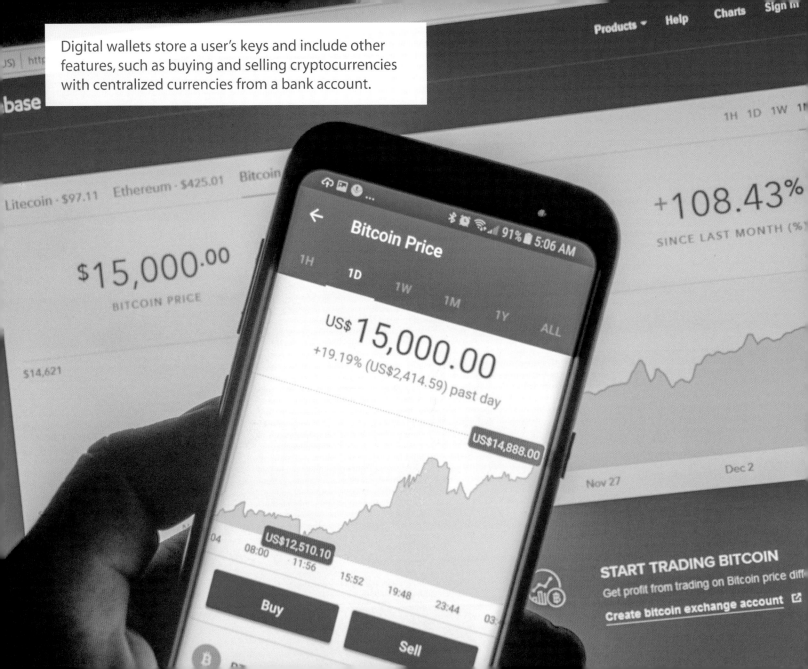

Digital wallets store a user's keys and include other features, such as buying and selling cryptocurrencies with centralized currencies from a bank account.

transaction, and as long as John's private key is safe, the two bitcoins will now be his money.

Keeping It Safe

At this point, the miners take over. The new block from the miners will make the trade between Jane and John official. Miners solve complex mathematical calculations that result in a block that is added to the blockchain of transactions. Before a block is added to the blockchain, other miners verify that all the transactions in that block are valid. This is done to verify that Jane did not send those two bitcoins to more than one person. When this is done, the transaction is officially added

DID YOU KNOW?

Private keys can be represented in many ways. One of the most common is a string of sixty-four characters zero through nine or A through F. This combination makes guessing someone's private key nearly impossible.

to the blockchain. It becomes a verified transaction in the public ledger. The blockchain is one of the safety features of cryptocurrency.

Miners are a critical component of cryptocurrency systems.

Despite its safety features, cryptocurrency is not foolproof. Anytime private keys are stored online, they can be stolen. Even the best security systems may fail. So, many people choose to store their keys to their wallets offline. Some people use desktop wallets. They create a file with the keys in it. A user can store the file on a USB drive. Any wallet stored on an offline device is called a cold wallet. Some people also make paper copies of the private keys.

Crypto Debit Cards

Crypto debit cards are a new innovation. They make it easier to pay for things quickly using digital currency. Before, people had to use an app or go to a digital exchange. Debit cards are improving this process. They automatically exchange the currency. Some are prepaid debit cards or debit cards linked directly to the user's digital wallet. And they work on card scanners stores already use for credit card purchases. Many experts believe the debit cards will make cryptocurrency a more common payment method.

CHAPTER 3

Crypto Challenges

In 2017, an information technology (IT) worker named James Howells made an unusual request. He asked the city council in his hometown of Newport, Wales, for permission to dig in the landfill. Howells wanted to find an item that he had mistakenly thrown away four years earlier. The item was now worth millions of dollars—if he could only find it.

DID YOU KNOW?

Bitcoins that have been mined but have not circulated for 18 months or longer are referred to as "zombie coins." Zombie coins make up an estimated 30 percent of all bitcoins in circulation. Most of these coins are considered lost. This means no one has the private key for them.

Users who store their digital wallets and keys on a hard drive should keep the hard drive if they get rid of the computer.

What Howells hoped to recover was the hard drive from his Dell laptop. In February 2009, Howells had begun to mine bitcoins, making him one of the earliest miners. He gradually amassed 7,500 bitcoins and stored his public and private keys in a digital wallet on his laptop's hard drive. At the time, the bitcoins were worth only a fraction of a cent. But Howells had hoped that his bitcoins would grow in value.

"After I had stopped mining, the laptop I had used was broken into parts and sold on eBay," Howells said. "However, I

Computer security is a concern for cryptocurrency users and exchanges. Hackers can attempt to steal private keys.

kept the hard drive in a drawer at home knowing it contained my Bitcoin private keys, so that if Bitcoin did become valuable one day I would still have the coins I had mined."

Unfortunately, the hard drive accidentally ended up in the garbage during a cleaning spree. Along with it went the bitcoins, estimated to be worth $127 million. Despite the value, Howells did not receive permission to dig in the landfill. His millions of dollars in bitcoins remain buried.

Howells is not alone in his quest to find lost keys. It is a problem unique to digital currencies. Forgotten passwords and lost hardware means users are locked out of their own accounts. There is no central agency, such as a bank, to help users recover funds. It is just one of the challenges users are discovering as digital currency enters the mainstream.

Hackers

Hackers are people who gain access to other people's computers and networks. They often do this illegally. Hackers pose another real and dangerous threat to users of digital currencies. Hackers are well known for targeting cryptocurrency exchanges. These exchanges manage a large and tempting pool of money. They can place transactions buying and selling on behalf of clients. In 2018, more than 200 exchanges operated around the world. The ten largest exchanges together

Changes in Value

Cryptocurrency is not stable like the US dollar or the euro. Instead, its value changes greatly from day to day. In December 2017, one bitcoin was equal to $19,783.03. Nine months later, the value had dropped. One bitcoin was equal to only $6,542.78. This large value shift makes using cryptocurrency a challenge. Users constantly risk losing the value of their money. And many businesses do not want to accept a payment that may be worth less the next day. But some investors like this value change. They hope to buy cryptocurrencies at a low price. When the price increases, they can sell their cryptocurrency. The difference can be a profit for aggressive investors.

Mt. Gox held press conferences after it was hacked and after a court hearing involved the former CEO.

averaged more than $6.5 billion in trades each day in 2018.

The first massive **hack** of a cryptocurrency exchange occurred on an exchange called Mt. Gox. It was the world's largest Bitcoin exchange. By February 2014, it was handling 70 percent of all Bitcoin trades. But in February 2014, Mt. Gox leaders made an announcement. They stopped all trade on the exchange. A **leak** revealed that hackers had stolen 744,408 bitcoins that belonged to customers. They had also taken 100,000 bitcoins that belonged to the exchange. Mt. Gox was forced to declare bankruptcy.

In the following months, Mt. Gox leaders found that 200,000 of the stolen bitcoins had not actually been transferred.

The private keys had been held in files that hackers had not touched. But the remaining 644,408 missing bitcoins remained lost. The total loss was valued at $450 million. In the following years, users of online forums put forward theories about the hack. But investigators have never uncovered exactly how it happened.

The next major cryptocurrency theft occurred in January 2018. Hackers attacked an exchange called Coincheck. They stole more than $500 million in a digital currency called NEM. This was one of the largest thefts in history. To stop the thieves from spending the money, NEM programmers created a tracking system. It alerts potential buyers that the currency is stolen. But the hackers found ways to **launder** the currency and continued to spend it.

 DID YOU KNOW?

Between 2011 and 2018, hackers succeeded in 56 separate cyberattacks on digital currencies. The total amount stolen during that period is estimated at $1.63 billion.

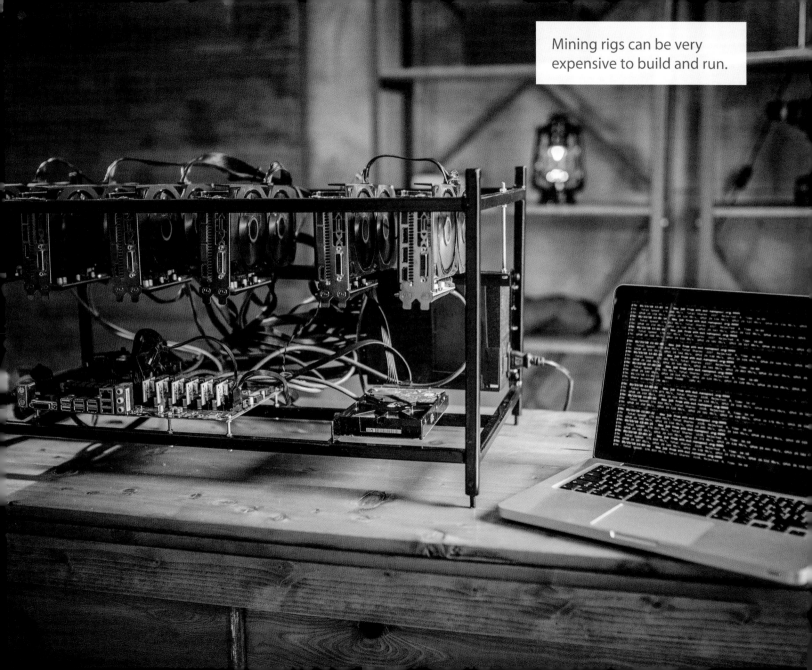

Mining rigs can be very expensive to build and run.

A Big Impact

Electricity and computer hardware are another issue in the world of digital currency. The use of these resources is greatest during the mining process. Miners use powerful hardware to solve puzzles. To solve these puzzles, miners must produce a "proof of work." This is basically a complicated math problem. Often, miners use several computers at once. Doing so increases their chance of solving the problem first and earning valuable cryptocurrency in return.

Running thousands of these powerful computers uses lots of electricity. In 2018, mining for cryptocurrency was

Mining Rigs

Many miners use a computer system that has only one job: to mine cryptocurrency. The computer system does not perform any other tasks. It is called a mining rig. Mining rigs are expensive. An entry-level rig costs between $1,000 and $10,000, depending on the computer's power. Mining rigs also require special software that solves complex math problems quickly. Some people have turned their mining rigs into businesses. AntPool is a Chinese company that pools lots of mining rigs together. It is one of the biggest mining operations in the world.

estimated to use 0.5 percent of the entire world's energy. That breaks down to approximately 70 terawatt-hours per year. That is more electricity than the entire country of Switzerland uses in one year.

Sometimes, the electricity comes from renewable resources, such as solar or wind power. But in most cases, it does not. It usually comes from fossil fuels that are burned to create electricity. This pollutes the environment. And these fuels are not renewable.

Electricity is not the only resource mining uses in large quantities. Hardware used for mining has also grown in demand recently. Graphics processing units (GPUs) have become hot-ticket items for miners. In the past, gamers were the primary market for these computer parts. GPUs are used to display high-quality 3D graphics in games. But when the cryptocurrency Ethereum grew in value, miners realized that GPUs were good at solving the math problems involved in mining. When Bitcoin mining gained popularity, GPUs did, too. They became nearly impossible to find and rose steeply in price.

DID YOU KNOW?

In 2017, cryptocurrency miners spent $776 million on more than 3 million GPUs.

The Dark Web

Another challenge holding back the growth of cryptocurrency is its association with the dark web. The dark web is a part of the internet. But it can only be accessed with special software. The software keeps people's identities and their transactions secret. It's nearly impossible to trace anything that happens on the dark web. As a result, many illegal activities occur there. People can buy drugs or weapons. Some people also sell bank account passwords and stolen credit card numbers.

People who deal on the dark web want to remain unknown. They do not want to be connected to any crimes they commit there. Cryptocurrency makes this

Programs like Tor help people access the dark web.

easier. It allows two people to exchange money and goods without worrying that a bank or the police could track the money. Their true identities also remain completely unknown to each other. For these reasons, cryptocurrency has been closely associated with the dark web and crime.

The dark web has tarnished the reputation of cryptocurrency. But this

Law enforcement works to track down illegal activity on the dark web.

has not been enough to keep people away. Many law-abiding citizens are still interested in the technology behind cryptocurrency. As a result, cryptocurrency's future remains bright as people seek to use it in new and creative ways.

DID YOU KNOW?

In June 2018, the US Department of Justice released the results of a year-long operation on the dark web. During that time, officials arrested 35 people and seized $23.6 million. Nearly $20 million was stored as cryptocurrency or as computers used for mining.

CHAPTER 4

Speculating the Future

When Satoshi Nakamoto introduced the world to Bitcoin in 2009, it had limited appeal. Most of the people interested in it worked in IT. But that has changed recently. Today, interest in cryptocurrency is growing. Financial investors and mainstream consumers alike are involved in digital currencies.

Some experts believe increased digital currency use will spark something called a network effect. This effect is similar to a snowball rolling down a hill. It grows in size as it gains speed. As more people use digital currency, more people will want to try it themselves, and more businesses will accept it as a form of payment. As the network of users and businesses grows, the network has more value for everyone.

Massive changes to currency systems are slow. And their effects are hard to predict. Aleh Tsyvinski is an economics professor at Yale University. He studies cryptocurrency and what its impact on the

The increase in popularity of cryptocurrencies has made them easier to use. This, in turn, makes them more attractive to potential users.

future may be. "I think it's actually going to pose more threat not to government money, but to companies like Visa, MasterCard, major banks, maybe other industries—the finance industry," says Tsyvinski. "That's where the destruction is going to be." As a new monetary system becomes available, the existing companies that work in financing, loans, and money could be affected. If a lot of people pull their money out of a bank to use cryptocurrencies, the bank might not have enough money to make new loans. Since interest and fees are how banks make a profit, this could put the bank out of business.

A New Option

With that destruction comes opportunity. This is especially true in countries where the local currency is weak and does not hold its value. Imagine, for example, that $10 could buy four candy bars one week. The next week, the same $10 may only buy two candy bars. In countries with unstable currencies, residents worry about how they will be able to support themselves.

In the past, people had few options. Exchanging their local currency for a different nation's currency was the only choice. But cryptocurrency changed that entirely. People are now exchanging their local currency for cryptocurrency. This strategy is not without risks, though.

Cryptocurrency can also be unstable. But for many people, it is still safer than their local currency.

Between May 2017 and May 2018, Venezuela's currency, the bolívar, nosedived in value. Prices in Venezuela rose by nearly 24,600 percent. As a result, Venezuelans turned to cryptocurrency

When the bolívar value plummeted, many people in Venezuela began buying as much food as they could. Some parts of the country started rationing food.

in increasing numbers. Their country is becoming a massive experiment in how cryptocurrency might help or hurt failing economies.

"Here in Venezuela, where we are in the midst of a political and economic crisis, cryptocurrency is not a game. It is a safeguard of value and protection against the hyperinflation of our own

Inflation can make a currency worth much less than it was.

Trusting Tech

In countries with weak economies, cryptocurrency may help people avoid losing their life savings. They only need access to the internet. But that does not mean everyone is rushing to exchange their traditional currency. Many people across the world do not have access to a secure internet connection. Many people also distrust a currency that exists only virtually. Numbers on a computer screen are not the same as coins in a pocket. This distrust and lack of access is slowing cryptocurrency's growth.

Blockchains are good for securely verifying data.

currency, the bolívar," said Venezuelan tech writer José Rafael Peña Gholam. "In other countries, many people see bitcoin as a speculative and volatile asset. But in Venezuela, bitcoin fulfills its main function of being a currency that is not issued by a central bank nor controlled by a government, and thus is more trusted than the bolívar."

New Uses

Digital currency's impact goes beyond money. Blockchain is the backbone of cryptocurrency. This technology has the potential for widespread use in the future. Blockchain technology is not limited to cryptocurrencies. It can be used in a variety of industries. Many business leaders are interested in how they can

DID YOU KNOW?

Blockchain technology is growing quickly. But it still faces an uphill battle. A 2017 survey by the bank HSBC revealed that 59 percent of people across the globe had never heard of blockchain technology. Of those who had heard of it, 80 percent did not understand how it worked.

apply blockchain technology to their own companies.

At its most basic, blockchain technology is a way to process and store transactions. The transactions can be with currency, but they can also involve any kind of data. As long as information changes hands, blockchains can help verify the transaction. Blockchain has many benefits. It is resistant to fraud. And it can process a large volume of transactions in a short amount of time. The result is a verified record of data's movement over time. This technology could prove useful in many industries, from ride sharing to medical records.

The state of Illinois is a leader in working on applying blockchain technology. The state began a **pilot program** in 2017. It uses blockchain to track a person's identity. The program

DID YOU KNOW?

The number of blockchain transactions for cryptocurrencies is on the rise. On March 18, 2017, analysts noted 206.12 million transactions in a single day. Exactly a year later, that number had grown to 305.61 million transactions.

begins when a baby is born. He or she is issued a birth certificate on a blockchain. This includes data such as the baby's legal name, birth date, and blood type. As the child grows, new identity information can be added to the blockchain.

The identity data remains encrypted. A person needs to give permission before allowing anyone to access their data. If this system becomes fully operational, it could make many government processes smoother. Imagine that a person wants to get a driver's license, for example. He or she must provide documents, such as a birth certificate. With blockchain, that step could be skipped. The department could instantly access the birth certificate on the state's blockchain.

DID YOU KNOW?

Cryptocurrencies are growing at a rapid pace. In 2013, only 40 cryptocurrencies existed. By 2017, that number had jumped to 1,237. That is an increase of 3,083 percent in just four years.

Other Uses

Other groups are experimenting with blockchains, too. The United Nations uses blockchain technology to track aid and deliver it to **refugees**. WePower is working to allow people to buy and sell renewable energy with each other directly using blockchain. Everledger is working to apply blockchain technology to luxury goods. It would track the movement of diamonds, wine, and even art. Follow My Vote is testing how blockchain technology could help people cast, track, and count votes.

Even the United Nations is finding a way to use blockchain technology.

Blockchain technology holds promise in many fields. And as cryptocurrency grows, it may change the way people around the world spend money. But right now, many people are still unsure about using cryptocurrencies. It will take time for the currency and its technology to prove themselves to the world as safe and useful. No one is sure what exactly it will take to prove to people that cryptocurrency is safe. But many people believe blockchain technology and digital currency will influence the world economy for decades to come.

Nodes

Nodes are one of the most important parts of blockchain technology. A node is one device on an online service. All of the nodes together form a network. Large cryptocurrencies, such as Bitcoin, have hundreds of thousands of nodes. Each node stores a copy of the blockchain. For someone to hack into the blockchain would require them to change the data on 51 percent of the nodes. Doing this on hundreds of thousands of separate computers is next to impossible. The node system is one of the reasons that blockchain is so secure.

circulation (SUR-cue-lay-shun): passing from person to person.

fraud (FRAWD): an act intended to deceive or cheat.

hack (HAK): an illegal accessing of a computer or network.

ingots (ING-gut): metal that is molded into a shape that is easy to carry.

launder (LAWN-dur): to transfer money illegally and hide its original source.

leak (LEEK): information from a secret source that has been made public.

ledger (LEH-jur): account books that keep a record of deposits and withdrawals.

pilot program (PIE-lut PROH-gram): a trial program.

refugees (REH-few-geez): people fleeing their homeland to escape danger.

transaction (tran-ZAK-shun): trading goods, money, or services.

verify (VER-uh-fy): to prove the truth of a fact or event.

FOR MORE INFORMATION

Books

Bitsy Kemper. *Growing Your Money*. Minneapolis, MN: Lerner Publications, 2015. This book gives readers information about saving and investing money.

Matthew Anniss. *Understanding Computer Networks*. Chicago, IL: Capstone Heinemann Library, 2015. This book takes a look at the different kinds of computer networks and how they work.

Megan M. Gunderson. *Banks and Banking*. Minneapolis, MN: Abdo Publishing, 2013. This book teaches kids about banks, interest, and loans.

Websites

Blockchain for Kids (https://lisk.io/academy/blockchain-basics/blockchain-for-kids) Learn more about blockchains and peer-to-peer transactions.

What Is the Blockchain? (https://www.kidscodecs.com/what-is-the-blockchain/) Discover how blockchains securely record information.

"Bitcoin" Is a New Type of Money (https://teachingkidsnews.com/2013/04/24/1-bitcoin-is-a-new-type-of-currency/) Learn more about bitcoin and how it's different from other types of money.

Kate Conley has been writing nonfiction books for children for more than ten years. When she's not writing, Conley spends her time reading, drawing, and solving crossword puzzles. She lives in Minnesota with her husband and two children.